Balboa Press books may be ordered through booksellers or by contacting:

Balboa Press
A Division of Hay House
1663 Liberty Drive
Bloomington, IN 47403
www.balboapress.com
1-(877) 407-4847

Because of the dynamic nature of the Internet, any web addresses or links contained in this book may have changed since publication and may no longer be valid. The views expressed in this work are solely those of the author and do not necessarily reflect the views of the publisher, and the publisher hereby disclaims any responsibility for them.

The author of this book does not dispense medical advice or prescribe the use of any technique as a form of treatment for physical, emotional, or medical problems without the advice of a physician, either directly or indirectly. The intent of the author is only to offer information of a general nature to help you in your quest for emotional and spiritual well-being. In the event you use any of the information in this book for yourself, which is your constitutional right, the author and the publisher assume no responsibility for your actions.

Any people depicted in stock imagery provided by Thinkstock are models, and such images are being used for illustrative purposes only.
Certain stock imagery © Thinkstock.

ISBN: 978-1-4525-4212-6 (e)
ISBN: 978-1-4525-4213-3 (sc)

Printed in the United States of America

Balboa Press rev. date: 03/29/2012

To My Grandmother: Yaye Diodio Ndiaye

Contents

PART 3

Introduction

What makes people great is their ability to be in contact consciously or unconsciously with some eternal truths and open our eyes to universal laws that have always existed.

They live it, put it into practice, prove it. And they try to tell us that this law will work the same way for you as it did for them, because a law by definition applies to everybody, every time, everywhere. We are used to focus on the achievement of great men but often forget to seek to understand the mindset that gave birth to these "miracles", how they approached life.

What I find interesting about all the great men I have studied, is how they try, and always succeed to give back to the world the wisdom they got from the universe, what they have learned from their own experience, their legacy. They try to say in few words experiences of a lifetime.

- When the Power of Love overcomes the Love of Power, the world will know Peace.

- Be the change you want to see.

- Do to others as you would like them do to you.

- Injustice anywhere is a threat to justice everywhere.

- When you change the way you look at things, the things you look at change.

- Ask not what your Country (the Universe) can do for you, but what you can do for your Country.

- Live as if you were to die tomorrow, learn as if you were to live forever.

- I am the Greatest (believe in yourself)

- Be like water (be flexible)

- All that we are is the result of what we have thought.

When we hear these words there is something in us that react to their energy. We know it to be true just like if it was our own statement, our own life experience, our own wisdom.

Because the truth is universal and the same wisdom that these people were connected to and came out with these truths, is the same wisdom that is in every human being.

They discover (not create), something that was there before them and will be there after them.

The truth does not belong to the one that discovered it or said it first, if you understood it, you too can experience it. But you have to experience the truth of it in your own life.

Sometime we can get misled by thinking that these are just "beautiful words", but when you take time to study them, you will find out that they are profound truths, and that their truthfulness and their depth is what makes them beautiful. After all the truth is God and God is beautiful.

You don't need to be famous or special to experience the universal laws or the eternal truths. They are open for every single one of us to discover but we have to experience them because until then, they will just be concept in our mind.

What I call God in this book; some call it the Divine Power, the Source, the Divine Matrix, the Organizing Intelligence, the Container; is available and accessible in all time, in all places, to everyone unconditionally and everyone equally.

Family Heritage

The experience of my life led me to the realization of what I call "The Simple Truth".

I was born and I grew up in Senegal, in West Africa, into a Muslim family. My grandmother was the head of the family spiritually and financially. She was not feared, but respected and not only for her age but for her wisdom.

She was not interfering very much in the lives of others, but when she did it was always to share her life experience and to talk about ethics, morals and doing the right thing.

She was very religious, talking about God and the importance of faith most of the time.

She was very loving and always helping the needy, and I remember that whenever she was giving away money to people, she made sure no one saw it or noticed that the person came to ask for help.

She was very devoted to her religious practices, she would stop everything she was doing, when it was time for the five daily prayers. In fact she was not doing much, mostly just being, and it seemed that she was in a constant state of contemplation, very present in the moment. She would try to fast even when she was sick during the month of Ramadan and she spoke of her trip to Mecca, long before I was born, with nostalgia and pride.

My mother was different from my grandmother, but not in essence. Her, I would call spiritual and not religious. She was not constant in a daily prayers, she did not fast everyday during the holy month of Ramadan, but she already embodied the qualities that these acts of devotion are supposed to awaken in a human being. She was an ocean of love which I could just dive in whenever I wanted. She was known to be the peacemaker in the family, she could not stand two people not talking to each other, she would do whatever she could to create an atmosphere of joy, to release the energy of anger in the house, and she would not be at peace until they become friends again. When I quarrelled with my little sister, we both had to apologize and forgive each other, it did not matter who did what. Her generosity to others was sometime too much for me to bear in that age, because I could ask her for money to buy a soccer ball or a new pair of shoes and she could refuse me and the next moment I could hear someone thank her for the money she or he just received. And when I confronted her with anger, She would reply that this person needed the money for something more important than my "luxury problems" as she called them.

Charity, to give to the poor is something that she taught me very early. There was an old blind man who was always accompanied by his granddaughter, going to people houses every morning to beg for food, money, clothes, just anything. My mother always gave me something to give him. He became my friend, and everyday when he arrived, he would just call my name and I would run with enthusiasm to give him something, and he would pray for me and for the whole family.

My grandmother told me that when my mother was small, at the age of six, seven years, she used to go every Friday in a corner of the house at a specific time in the afternoon and seemed to be engaged in some activities. One day she asked her why she always leaves everything she was doing every time that moment came. She never answered, and when she was forced to speak, she told her that a group of Angels used to come and play with her every Friday afternoon. They came by wagon and they called her name, and they told her never to tell anyone about their visit. She has never seen them again after she spoke to my grandmother about it.

If there was a quality to be learned from my mother during my childhood, it would be peace.

She loved peace and thought that the way to peace is forgiveness, always forgiveness.

And from my grandmother, it would be: to do the right thing.

Glimpses Of Religion

When I was six and ready to start school, my mother insisted that I go to private catholic school instead of the normal public school in Senegal, because they had the best education system in the country with the best results. My grandmother made no objection on me going to a catholic school. But at the same time I was going to Koranic school, twice a week with a private teacher to learn the Koran and the Islamic traditions. This was not unusual in Senegal with 94% Muslims, 5% Christians and 1% domestic religions. Coexistence and religious tolerance in Senegal is an example and an inspiration for the world. In fact most of my schoolmates were Muslims and were going to Koranic school at the same time.

At school the education system was French and purely academic, the priests and the teachers treated all the students the same way regardless of religion.

There was a small sculpture of a man on a cross in all classrooms and teachers who were Christians used to start the day by a prayer and those who wanted to repeat after them could do it, but no one was forced to. And I used to do it sometime when I felt for it, just like my other classmates, Muslims and Christians, we didn't even know the meaning of what we were saying.

The man on the cross seemed very strange but very special and his name sounded familiar.

We also had Muslim teachers and you could not tell the difference. There was a large Church at the school and once a week they had a ceremony called "Mass" and it was open for anyone.

The ceremony took place after school and I tried once to go into the church before my mother came to take me, it was a very special place I thought, with pictures and sculptures of a man, a woman, a cross and many songs and rituals. It was a beautiful experience, and the first time I told my mother and my grandmother that I went into a church, (I was the first person in my family to visit a church) they asked how it was and how it felt like. They did not prohibit me to go there again, and I did it several times more with some classmates Muslims and Christians. I did not place any special value on it, I was just six years old and did not know much about religion; this was my school, the man on the cross was called Jesus: a Prophet and a very important one in Islam my parents told me, and the son of God or God Himself from what I understood from the Christians. But to me there was no difference in that age: a Prophet, God son, God, it was all part of the same.

Religion both from school and at home gave me the same message: that there is a higher being called God who created us and the Universe, but that I thought, was something to think about when you grow up.

I never heard my family criticize or say a bad word about Christianity or Jesus and at school they never taught me anything bad about Islam. In fact the only difference between Muslims and Christians, I used to hear growing up in Senegal, was that: Christians believe that Jesus was the son of God and Muslims believe that he was a Prophet, because the Koran say so.

3

◄◦►

Awakening Of The
Seeker In Me

At the age of 16, I was suddenly very interested in trying to understand the big questions of existence, the meaning of everything: birth, life, death, the Universe. How to find the mystical being behind creation?

The arrogance of science pretending to be the absolute truth and tool to understand the universe and rejecting all other knowledge and belief as superstitions and ignorance could not satisfy me. Because I could feel that it was more to life and reality than what my five senses and my raison were telling me. I could not prove it to myself, as Newton and Darwin have proven their scientific theories, but it was a knowing at the core of my being, and as an African born and raised in Senegal, I could hear, feel and accept that paranormal was one aspect of reality, and that supernatural was a word in human language for "natural" experiences that we can not yet understand.

I grew up witnessing People accomplish miraculous healings and metaphysical experiences that defy all laws of physics.

In my search for answers I read Descartes, Jean Paul Sartre, Renan and many other French philosophers because of our French education system in Senegal, and I was not convinced. I saw philosophy as a labyrinth of thoughts that produces more questions than answers, and the entire wisdom of philosophy as I saw it then, was in the statement that says, "Science without conscience is the ruin of the soul".

I saw science and philosophy as tools to try to understand the effects, and I was interested in the causes. So I was attracted to religion with the feeling that the secret of life must be there hidden.

My grandmother was a big influence to my interest in Islam by her way of being. She always had that "something", an inner power. Her presence reminded me of God.

My seeking journey led me to a Sufi mystic in Senegal called Cheick Ahmadou BAMBA, who lived in this earth from 1853 to 1927. He wrote prodigious quantity of poems and tracts on meditation, rituals, work, and Koran study. He was a poet, a monk and a religious leader. He politically led a pacifist struggle against the French colonialism without waging war. He advocated non violence, learning, work, and alignment with God.

Cheikh Ahmadou Bamba became my spiritual teacher, and he made me understand, the power of Faith. His life and achievements proved to me that if you believe enough you can accomplish miracles. I started reading both Islamic and Christian spiritual books, I read the Koran, and the Bible (which was very unusual for a Muslim to do at that age, if at all), but I believe that a ground for an open mind in spirituality was already in me from my catholic school experience.

I realized later that I read everything just to find unconsciously, evidences about the power of Faith, and it was not important where I got them from. I even found very early that the difference between the Koran and the Bible was not much, (the essence was the same) it was mostly about the personality of Jesus and the interpretation of the Trinity. And I was more interested in his message, the depth and meaning of his parables and specially his faith, that if he was only a Prophet or God son. In fact I never had a problem about the concept of the "son of God" because I have always believed that we are all "sons" and "daughters" of our creator.

In fact the only thing I was interested in was to discover the Creator, and furthermore there was no difference, from my understanding, in the teachings of Jesus and those of Muhammad, (peace be upon both of them). The one thing I needed in order to know and experience God according to my knowledge of the Bible and the Koran, and my spiritual teacher confirmed it to me, was faith.

4

—◄O►—

Discovering Faith

When I turned 20, my grandmother died, and that day something I could not explain but I could feel happened to me. During the last years of her life, she was very hard on me about ethics, self discipline, the importance of the daily prayers, doing the right thing, more than anyone else in the family. I was the only one she would use her energy to preach and to make sure I was doing the right thing. The day she passed away, I was in the car that took her to the hospital and she was unconscious for some days. I remember that I had a strange feeling when I held her hand in the car because it was the first time I experienced the feeling of someone in that state of being.

At the hospital I was allowed to be in the room before the arrival of the Doctor, then we were told to leave. I saw her lying on her hospital bed and it was the last time I saw grand- ma.

When I came home, I was very sad and quite, I went to make my ablution for prayer, and just when I started to pray, I heard my mother crying and screaming that grand-ma passed away.

To my greatest surprise, I continued my prayer with a serenity that I never felt before. I was not sad, not angry, I was in total surrender. The next day when she was buried, I cried, it felt like I lost my best friend. I regretted to not have spent more time with her, and listened to her wisdom. As they say in Senegal, "In Africa when an old person dies, it's like a library has burned".

However I sincerely believe that at the time of her death when her soul was leaving her body she gave something to me, she "touched" me in one way or another. In that very moment when I was praying and heard my mother, I know that my normal reaction would have been to "cut" the prayer or at least to do it quickly and come and comfort my mother or be part of the sorrow, but something was going through me, I could feel it, it was not "me".

And since that day, is just like "I held the flame" after her. I became more serious in my practices, and I reminded everyone when it was time to pray, and about God.

I later understood that she was preparing me all her life, to not let the light fades when she passed away. She made me feel God.

My appetite for reading and seeking knowledge was growing stronger, and I embraced silence often, and when I did not read, I contemplated nature or listened to people. You can learn a lot by contemplating nature but is amazing what you can learn by listening to people.

It seemed that life was a teacher speaking to me at all time, and that I had to be quiet and listen carefully.

My family and my friends thought I was weird. We have to understand that in Africa, solitude and silence is not very much supported by the traditions. And I used to hear that it was dangerous to be away from people at my age, because I could go crazy, and that only mature people should do it because they have the wisdom to confront the evil spirits who might find them in their solitude.

But I did not care about what people said or thought about me, I knew I had discovered something. In silence I found a companion and the most fulfilling experience so far in my life.

I felt whole in solitude and silence.

One day a book came to me that would shake my religious beliefs and my entire life.

The name of the book was: "The Power of your Subconscious Mind", by Joseph Murphy.

I remember that it was the title of the book that caught my eye and appealed to me.

This book confirmed to me the power of belief, and for the first time I understood that the power was also in me and all of us. I realized that creating miracles in our life was not the privileges of some Prophets or saints, but that everyone could access this power.

But the revolution for me was his statement that it was not the thing you believe in that creates the miracle, but the act of believing. It was very radical and disturbing to me, but at the same time I found it to be the missing link. It was the best explanation I had to why God answered prayers to people from different faith and even non- religious people.

It made a lot of sense to me, it was an answer to a big question but at the time, it raised even a bigger question: "Does it matter then where you get the belief from?" I think I knew the answer. Because if you can accept that it is the act of belief and not what you believe in that creates the miracle, then it is obvious that it does not matter where you got the belief from.

But it was so radical and revolutionary, even seemed non- religious to me, that the idea had to make his way through different barriers and layers of religious traditions, taboos, and misinterpretation to reach and settle into my subconscious.

5

Experiencing Miracle

After a long internal conflict, I was totally convinced of my new discovery and I realized even that it was not in contradiction with the spirit of the Koran or the Bible. The saying: "if you tell a mountain to move and believe enough, it will move", was something I believed in the very first time I heard it, I had no evidence in fact my mind told me the opposite. I must have been very little but it sounded true.

I was very happy to know now that the power to create miracle was not given to some few, but to me too, and I decided to test God. I remember I said: "God you said that if I believe enough I can get anything I want, you know my dream is to go to Europe and play football, I know I have a knee injury, and I know I don't see how, but you are God and I believe – I am waiting".

I became a magnetized person. I started to notice what I then called "the hidden side of things".

I saw God everywhere, not only in living things, but even in inanimate things, I saw that there was no coincidence, that there was in fact a great perfection and harmony in creation.

The daily experience of life became more important that the outcome, playing football became pleasure instead of a means to become someone. Life was opening his secrets to me and I was writing down most of my experiences and my insights.

I remember to have considered the idea of renouncing all earthly ambition of success, and it was the desire to please my mother and to give a decent life to my girl friend at the time that kept me away from that.

After less than a year, an uncle of mine who lived in Sweden came to holiday in Senegal and I went to meet him at the airport, and I remember the first word he said to me was: "I will not go back without you," and so it was, God kept his promise. This was everything to me, because God has shown His power, which is the power of belief. And for me it was as big as any miracle I ever read in the Scriptures, because this was my own experience, and there is nothing more powerful than a personal experience. I know how impossible the situation was then and how it came to existence.

I realized that miracles were as objective and real as gravity. It was no longer a belief but a knowing. From that personal experience, the voice of my rational mind that used to say to me sometime that the miracle stories in the Scriptures may just be legends to make people believe in God, has to be defeated. It has to give up because God gave me a evidence, not something I read somewhere, not someone else's experience, but my own (something I went through). I used to call God, "The one who keeps his promises" and I asked: " Lord consider each beat of my heart as thanks giving" because if you grant me that, I will be sure that I thank you as you deserve, when I sleep and when I forget.

I started to think that if I could manifest this, I could manifest anything if I am faithful. It was scary. And now I thought, I had my own miracle that I will keep with me the rest of my life as a reminder.

Indeed miracles happen in our lives all the time, but we don't notice them, miracle is the nature and the essence of life. "Life is a miracle" is not only a beautiful saying it is indeed a profound truth. One can wonder about what it is that distracts us so much, that we don't spend the rest of our life in contemplation and wonder about the conception of human and animal life, the coming to existence of a flower and the vastness and complexity of the Universe? All creation is a miracle. Scientists are still struggling to understand the greatest mystery of life which is how everything came from nothing.

6

---⟨O⟩---

The Ghost Of Racism

In Europe, I continued my religious practices, I kept the five prayers of the day, fasted during the month of Ramadan and went to the Mosque as often as I could. But my encounter with some new realities such as racism at school and in my own football team, the religious intolerance, and the discussions I had with many Atheist (Scandinavia is in majority atheist), began to give me the impression that I don't belong here. I started to think in term of me and them. I saw disharmony and injustice in God's world. I became suspicious about human nature and started to identify with my race and my religion. I unconsciously sought allies. At school my friends were blacks, in my football team I would call them teammates and not friends, and on weekends after I played a game, I used to travel to another city to meet friends from the same country. The poison of racism slowly but surely penetrated me.

I listened to Malcolm X and tried to find evidence in the evilness of all white people and I found it everywhere because that was my expectation.

My state of mind became a state of anger, suspiciousness, defensiveness and often looking for a little act I considered racist to react. I think I unconsciously blamed God for allowing the evil of racism and I definitely blamed Christianity for being the root cause of white supremacy.

I read books and watched films about Slavery, the black struggle in America against racial segregation, the apartheid system in South Africa, colonialism in Africa and in other part of the world by whites. I searched for anything that could justify my anger and my idea of separation.

My faith and understanding of God decreased as I explored the labyrinth of man made evil.

Meanwhile my spiritual journey took a real setback, because I was trapped in the evil of the world and I allowed myself to be part of the problem instead of the solution. I began to lose my personal identity in favor of the group. In my view separation was obvious, it was meant to be.

Nevertheless my experience with the prejudices of racism did not last long, because after a while I began to notice that most whites in my team and school and others I knew were good people and some time better human beings than friends and even family member in Senegal. And that evidence of personal observation was creating a shift of perception.

Since childhood, I have always been a free spirit. I could listen but in the end I always decided what is good for me, and not what my parents or my teachers thought was good for me. I never gave anyone the authority to know what was best for me and I had many problems with my Father growing up, because he was the traditional father who knew best, who had been through life, done his mistakes and do not want you to do the same. He knew what you don't know and wants to guide you because he loves you and wants your best. I don't blame him for that, I even understand him. But my no spoken answer was: "I have to experience life myself". And I just couldn't compromise that, I was probably born with that attitude, and I came to understand later in life that my father had that similar attitude toward life and that I was just more extreme.

So when I changed perception, I decided to challenge all the ideas that were given to me about racism, and I saw directly that when I arrived in Europe, the first advice I received was to be "careful with the whites because they were very racist and very evil, and they do not see you as equal no matter how good you are". And of course I was unconsciously collecting evidence to prove that assumption. And when you look for something, you will find it. In fact I could clearly see that people were mostly normal and good with me and the few times they behaved in a way a considered racist, could be when they were "just doing their job", following the rules of a particular system or just having a bad day. But those incidents I would see as an evidence of how true racism was everywhere, and never looked for the most part, because it would destroy the basis of the assumption.

Am I saying that there was no racism and that it was all in my head? Certainly not, what I am saying is that of course there is racism in Europe and it is a serious problem that should not be ignored, but is not a government policy. Nevertheless there are political parties that have racist agenda but they rarely come to power and it's a proof that a growing number of people in Europe have gone beyond racial prejudices. However there is a considerable number of people who still have racist considerations in their interaction with people of different race. But these are mostly unhappy human beings with their own issues in life, and need a "punching bag", or are ignorant or just "lost souls". And I think that the whites that have evolved from "the fear of the other," have a personal and a collective responsibility not to be passive against discrimination and injustice.

But the bottom line is that I must not allow what other people feel, think, say or do determine my experience. And the good news is that you can free yourself from other people negative influence by changing the way you look at things.

And in fact Malcolm X himself came to that conclusion after his pilgrimage to Mecca where he saw people of different race worshiping together in complete brotherhood.

To make a long story short, when I changed perception I saw that evil has no race, gender, or nationality. I then decided to change not only the way I saw things but the way I approached people, without prejudice, anticipation, judgment defensiveness. It was liberating, I felt free.

I was not carrying anymore the anger of slavery, segregation, apartheid, colonialism, the whole story of the black race. I still recall history, but only for the lessons it teaches me. I disassociated with the victim mentality. I didn't need to defend my colour, neither did I saw it to be any barrier for achieving anything. What I was and what I could be had nothing to do with my colour of skin or which part of the world I was born. I transcended race.

With that awareness, people reaction was surprising because even whites that had an unfriendly nature would be nice and respectful to me. The vibrations of no judgment that I expressed had no distinction of race or gender. I became more confident about myself and about life.

I discovered that I had a power that was given to me which was how I chose to see the world and that choice could change everything.

"All Men are created equal" made sense to me, because not only there is no superior race but it also means that all men were given the same power to create their life.

When you stop blaming you reclaim you power because you see your responsibility and that you can change it. The problem could still arise, I don't ignore it, but it could not affect me anymore because I became bigger than the problem. I stopped blaming God for human behaviour.

I reached that level of awareness only when I decided to see for myself and to judge from my own experience. Not someone else's experience regardless of the person greatness, or even from history regardless of its tragedy. What is true, I have to judge myself and the context must be now, not yesterday. I knew I got something with these two criteria of: "judging from my personal experience and not carrying with me the baggage of the past when I look at the present".

7

---⟨○⟩---

Reclaiming My Self After 9/11

My new insight: "To judge from personal experience and not to carry with you the baggage of the past when you look at the present" freed my mind from racism, but would I dare to apply it to religion that was more divisive factor than race. My argument was that the two were very different, and my religion was the true religion because God has said so in the Koran. Not a great person, a great thinker, or a Prophet, but God. So my personal understanding could not be used to interpret the words of God, and to defend my religion was an obligation because I was following God's will.

I knew within myself that to be true to myself, I had to question and unlearn many ideas and belief systems that were given to me and that I have never taken the time to question or dare to see in a new light. It was a conflict within me for what I felt to be true and what was said to be true.

9/11 was a turning point in my life because it gave rise to the collective consciousness, and brought to the surface, problems that were not addressed by our civilization.

If you look at 9/11 as an alien who just arrived on our planet, you will be faced with a scenario that shows aircrafts deliberately struck buildings after having been hijacked by people that had decided to kill themselves, and others. Many innocent people lost their lives just because they happened to be in a certain country, in a certain plane, in a particular building and at a certain time. The hijackers because of their state of mind were willing to die and to kill innocent people to make a statement. And people in that particular country decided to go and kill more innocent people, who just happened to be in a certain country, and had nothing to do with the hijackers and certainly not shared their ideas, to "say something back".

This was human behaviour in the year 2001, they used the noble and sacred name of religion, democracy, freedom and justice to act out their level of consciousness. As a Muslim it was clear to me that the "action" was against Islam as I understood it, and the "retaliation" had nothing to do with democracy, freedom, justice or weapons of masse destruction.

With 9/11, "evil" had a momentum, because hate was growing, suspiciousness, and prejudices were at work. The separating forces were stronger than ever, and fear was used to bring to the surface the dark side of our human nature. But whenever evil rises, goodness has to rise because the universe is always searching for a vehicle to channel a higher frequency so that we may evolve.

I remember one European leader statement: "to seize the moment and change the world".

Very enlightened words indeed because 9/11 was a wake- up call for the human race to see that the choices we make individually affects the collective consciousness of our planet and sooner or later some people will act it out. The events of 9/11 gave us an opportunity to stop and see as a family, were we have gone wrong and what these events were trying to tell us. Instead we started blaming, judging and focusing in the same ideas and feelings that created this consciousness in the first place. The action was not "in-spirit" neither was the reaction. We all carry so much "baggage", that we always see things from where we stands in the "cave" Socrates would say, not outside the cave where we can be free from ideology, prejudice, judgement, dogma and misinterpretation.

Only those who are "poor in spirit" can see the truth without distortion.

It was not only planes that were hijacked with the events of 9/11, but the spirit of Islam was hijacked with the action and the spirit of democracy, freedom and justice with the retaliation.

We are all to blame for the world we have created before and after 9/11. Some people carried the actions and the reactions but we are all responsible as part of the human family for what we didn't do before 9/11, when we allowed injustice and poverty in some part of the world that ultimately gave birth to extremist ideologies and desperate actions, and moderates believers fail to denounce radical interpretation of their faith. What we don't do shape the world as much as what we do, it is the silence of the good that allows evil to triumph.

It was I wake up call for me and I did wake up and saw how human beings used "Good and evil" just to act out their level of consciousness.

I then decided to reject any ideology and embark on a journey of "self discovery".

8

◀─○▶

The Call Of Spirit

To free one self from ideologies and belief systems is not an easy task and you have to be true to yourself and not any person or group. But when you are faithful to yourself, God will guide you to Him. It is an inner journey that has nothing to do with the concept of God, but rather with the experience of God.

On night, I dreamed that I had wings and flew with someone I carried in my arms. And I showed her something very important on the ground. But after a while I was forced to land and I could see that it was because my wings were dirty. The dream persisted for a long time and every time I woke up, the message was very clear: I had to clean my wings (my soul), I had to commit myself to practice what I knew to be true.

One evening lying on my bed, I had a strange experience it felt like "I" left my body, I was aware of my body without being in my body. I was two entities and the one that was not my body "watched" the rest. And for the first time in my life, I was aware of my heartbeat, the body aliveness, my thoughts and every cell of my being. I can not tell the time the experiment lasted, because I lost track of time. My eyes where closed throughout the experience and when I regained "consciousness", I knew directly that my life would never be the same.

That night I had deep thoughts and I made the connection with the dream that haunted me, it was clear to me that something greater than me was pushing me, directing me towards something.

The next day I decided to try to recreate the experience and a voice in my head told me that as a Muslim, the act of closing my eyes and trying to be in contact with whatever is, was associated with Buddhism and Eastern practices and not from the monotheistic religions of the Prophet Abraham(pbuh). But I ignored the voice and sat down, closed my eyes and started to go inward.

The experience was so fulfilling that I knew that I would be doing it the rest of my life. I started to meditate everyday and it added a depth into my daily prayers, I was more focus and more present in the moment while praying. I became more aware of the surrounding world, the aliveness of everything.

Then I decided to learn about Buddhism and Hinduism, and was immediately attracted to the truth of the spirit of their message: love, compassion, truth, self discipline, and self realisation.

I did not see any contradiction between those principles and the teachings of Islam, the topics of idols and reincarnation was the only difference and it could be subject to interpretation. But I was only interested on how to live in the best way, in harmony with life. I was searching for God and was open to everything, prejudice I knew was not to be trusted if you are a true seeker.

The more I studied these religions, the more I discovered that it was less about rules and punishment and more about human potential and self-realization. I did not hesitate to take with me and practice whatever appealed to me from these religions, I needed no permission from anyone or from anywhere to do so.

I followed my heart and his wisdom. I decided to never eat anything that has been killed, and I made meditation a daily practice. One of my friends was very confused and thought that I was leaving Islam and becoming a Buddhist, and about my attitude toward animals he thought it was a sanctification of animals which is to make them holy or worship them. But is actually the opposite of what he thought because the raison for me to not kill animals unnecessarily is because we humans have higher consciousness than animals and therefore should carry the responsibility to be kind and loving to them. And I tried to tell him that what I added in my spiritual journey was indeed in the depth of Islam but he could not see it. In fact the Prophet Muhammad (pbuh) meditated for many years in "Mount Hira" where he got the revelation that started his prophecy. He was not praying as we do now, but meditating. And it is said that he used to pray and meditate the second part of every night. So meditation was an integral part of the life of the Prophet Muhammad (pbuh).

About my decision not to eat what has been killed, it is in harmony with the vision of Islam. Because when you understand the spirit of the Koranic verses, the seeds of empathy for animal suffering and a sense of respect for all life exist by the recognition of the unity of creation and the mercy of God. All things belong to God and should be treated accordingly, and that's why it is forbidden for a Muslim to eat meat that is not "halal". One of the Ten Commandments given to the Prophet Moses was: "You shall not kill". It did not say, you shall not kill humans. There is a great wisdom in that commandment because all life is one. Leo Tolstoy ones said:" as long as we are killing animals, we will be killing each other too". And when the Prophet Muhammad (pbuh) returned to "Mecca", from is exile to "Medina", he said: "No living thing should be killed and no tree should be cut".

When you are true to yourself, then you can be freed of men made barriers and start to see similarity instead of differences. I saw clearly that all these religions had different rules and practices, but they all spoke about the same eternal principles of Love, Truth, Forgiveness, Compassion, Justice, Peace and Service. I thought then that there must be wisdom where the different rules and practices merge to focus in the same essence they shared, and it should be the spirit, because the rules and the practices are just doorways to the Spirit of the message. They are not the message.

Now the question became how to understand the spirit of the message? And the best way is to look at the Messenger, because he always embody the message, his way of being, his deeds, and his life story can tell you all about his message. Not the rules established after the messenger.

9

The Message from the Messenger
(THE SPIRIT OF THE MESSAGE OF ISLAM)

Religious scholars will argue that the only way to understand the message of a religion is through the holy book associated with that particular religion, in the case of Islam: that would be the Koran (words of God) and the "Hadiths" which are the sayings of the Prophet Muhammad (pbuh). And that's exactly where lies the problem, the words of God and the sayings of the Prophets can be understood but also misunderstood and misinterpreted because we do not have God's perfection. We are not all knowing, and we don't have the Prophets level of consciousness, their awareness to interpret literally their sayings, they speak in metaphors. The only humble way to understand a divine message is to try to grasp the spirit of the message and not the content, not the words. Because words are just pointers, that can lead you but they can mislead you to.

The Prophet Muhammad (pbuh) was once asked, "Who amongst us will be the first to follow you (die after you)? He said, "Whoever as the longest hand". So they started measuring their hands with a stick and a woman call Sauda turns out to have the longest hand. When a woman call Zainab bint Jahsh died first of all, in the (caliphate of Umar), amongst those that were present that day, they came to understand that the long hand was a symbol of practising charity.

Aisha the wife and very close friend of the Prophet Muhammad (pbuh) once said: "if you want to know the message of Islam, look at how the Prophet lived".

To know a tree, look at the fruits. If you want to know the spirit of Islam look at Muhammad (pbuh) and if you want to know the spirit of Christianity look at Jesus (pbuh), not their followers because they do not always represent the fruits of the tree.

THE MESSENGER OF ISLAM

Muhammad (pbuh) before the revelation was called "Al-Amin", the trust worthy. He was kind, loving, generous, and tender. He had a sense of social justice, he asked rich people that had slaves to free them as an act of faith, and he said that Men and Women are equal because in the side of God there is no colour or gender. He always identified with the disadvantage of society and was very compassionate. He lived among extremely backward people in a society in deep ignorance. He was like a diamond in a pile of stones.

This is what Gandhi said about Muhammad (pbuh): "I became more convinced that it was not the sword that won a place for Islam in those days in the scheme of life. It was the rigid simplicity, the utter self-effacement of the Prophet, the scrupulous regard for pledges, his intense devotion to his friends and followers, his intrepidity, his fearlessness, his absolute trust in God and in his mission.

The Spirit of the Message (from the messenger)

- There is only One God and Muhammad (pbuh) is his messenger.

- If you want to serve God serve people.

- "Jihad" is the constant struggle to better yourself.

- If you take one life you kill all humanity.

- We are all connected therefore all responsible.

- Do not be indifferent to injustice.

- Conserve your integrity in anytime.

- Unless you desire for your neighbor what you desire for yourself, you don't have faith.

- A man going to bed his belly full while his neighbor is hungry is not a Muslim.

- There is no difference in race, only the human race.

- An ink of a scholar is holier than a blood of a martyr.

- A man reading is handsome in the side of God. Learn and teach.

- Believe in all the Prophets.

- The people of the book must be respected by you, their book comes from God.

- God does not like, a man who consider himself above other man.

- Even I the Prophet of God do not know what will become of me.

10

———◄O►———

The Scriptures

Why the Scriptures have misled more than they have enlightened?

The Scriptures are considered to be the words of God, by whom he gave humans the knowledge, wisdom, guidance and commandments. But it is obvious when you look at the history of humanity and religion that we did not make good use of it, and the reason is simple.

We can consider the scriptures into four levels of comprehension.

- Words of God

- Deliver by a Prophet

- Written by an enlightened, inspired, or wise man.

- Interpreted by common people

The words of God must reflect his wisdom and consciousness, which is omnipotent, omniscient, and omnipresent, in summary perfection.

The message is delivered to the Prophet in different ways. The Prophet speaks the words of God from his state of mind, his own level of consciousness, he will only know what God wants him to know. When Prophets spoke God's words they were usually understood by few people even while alive when they spoke in front of them, because words have limited power. Is not always what they said, but what they pointed to, they could be understood or misunderstood naturally. Because men have different level of awareness, a different understanding and that is why Prophets had disciples, because they knew that these understood the spirit of their message better than the mass.

The Scriptures are written by enlightened or inspired men and not the prophet himself, it is from the person's own level of understanding. He is still telling the truth, but from his own level of awareness, which is not that of the Prophet or God.

Now the words of God which reflect his wisdom is delivered to Men by a messenger who is carefully chosen to live and teach the message. The message is written by inspired, enlightened or wises men, for "ordinary people" to understand. Wrong interpretation and misunderstanding of the word of God is inevitable.

Sometime learned men, rabbis, priests, imams, Gurus, scholars can spend their entire life trying to understand a verse or chapter in their holy book. To know about something does not mean that you understand it. A learned man is not equal to a wise man because wisdom you don't learn.

Knowledge is a collection of information and wisdom is the understanding of it.

When Jesus said to the learned of Israel that he could destroy the temple and rebuild it in three days, they did not understand him because they took it literally, but Jesus spoke about the body which is the temple of God. When he talked about being born again, they asked "how a human being could enter his mother's womb again". Jesus was talking about the spirit of man and not his form.

When the Prophet Muhammad(pbuh) said that, "he went to Jerusalem and from Jerusalem he was taken to the seven heavens and back to Medina in the same night", many of his followers were very sceptical because in their level of awareness which is limited with time and space that is impossible. But it is now known that, time and space, do not exist in a higher level of consciousness.

Prophets have been misunderstood throughout history because their words have been taken literally while they tried to explain a different reality to ordinary people with the limiting power of words.

The Scriptures should not be taken literally and should be treated with humility and wisdom.

No one should claim to know exactly what God mean when he communicates with us by words.

But "ordinary people" have been interpreting His words from their imperfect nature and acted upon it with divine authority. All the atrocities that man has inflicted to man (and animals for that matter) in the name of God have nothing to do with God. There is no one in human history who has been so falsely accused than God.

But let it be no mistake, God is Love. Anything other than love can not and does not come from God, and it does not matter how cleverly it is disguise.

So the way to avoid being misled by the content of the Scriptures is to try to grasp the spirit of it. Because just like with everything else, it is the spirit that holds it, is the spirit that makes it alive.

Without the spirit it ceases to exist. And the spirit of the Scriptures is nothing but the attributes of God: Love, Truth, Forgiveness, Peace, Justice, Compassion, Service etc...,

Anyone teaching anything other than that, is a victim of is own imperfection.

If you fail to seek the spirit of the Scriptures and want to interpret it literally, you will be subject to the observer effect.

11

───────◄○►───────

The Observer Effect

I could never imagine that science will give me the explanation of one of the most important question in my spiritual journey which is: "why do people with good intensions, really seeking God will read the same Koran that I read and still fail to see that God is only Love?"

According to Quantum theory," the moment we choose to observe something out of the infinite possibility that exist, the wave function of potentials collapses and a specific reality is formed".

Quantum physics is telling us that what the observer is bringing to the observation will determine the outcome of the experiment.

This was a revelation to me because I suddenly realized that of course if a person state of mind is that of resentment, unhappiness, bitterness, hate, jealousy, and dwelling on thoughts of an unjust world, when he opens the Koran, he will unconsciously look for raison and justification to reinforce all his thoughts, emotions and feelings. He will cleverly take words or sentences out of context, he will misinterpret and worse, he will filter out or simply ignore any verses that talk about forgiveness and love, just to be able to make his case.

When I open the Koran with my complete belief that God is only Love, I am probably doing the same thing, looking for evidences of God's love and obviously filtering out or ignoring the verses talking about punishment and revenge, to build my case. I still can see in the scriptures the destruction of "Sodom and Gomorra" and the deluge that destroyed those who did not followed the Prophet Noah, but that can't take away the conviction I have that God is love, Because I prefer to see the power of God in the harmony of the universe, in the beauty of a flower, in the wonder of the coming to being of humans an animals. I choose to see power in harmony and beauty and not in destruction.

Now if we take an alien with no "baggage" from our planet, he never heard about a book called Koran, never heard the word "God" and what we associate with it here on earth. This alien does not bring anything to what he is going to observe, no ideas, no beliefs. If you give him the Koran to read, the first thing he will encounter will be the beginning: "IN THE NAME OF THE MERCIFUL".

That beginning of the Koran is also the beginning of every chapter in the Koran.

Not the Powerful

Not the Wise

Not the Punisher

Even the verses that speak about punishment start with the "Merciful" not the "Punisher".

The Scriptures are trying to make us understand the ultimate nature of God at the very beginning, so that we may keep that in mind when we go about making our own interpretation.

The alien would not miss that but many of us do, because of our misconception of God.

We have created a "God" in our own image, and we still live in the old tradition that you have to "fear God".

But you don't have to fear God, you have to love God. Because fear and love are to different vibrations, in fact they are opposing vibrations. You can not love something you fear, it is not possible. You may respect it to avoid his punishment, but not love it in the pure sense of the word. And our relationship with our creator should be based on pure love, unconditional love.

What the Prophets and sages meant by fearing God was to fear doing things that keep us away from Him and prevent us from experiencing His love. Because when you are not in alignment with the spirit, and attributes of God, when you are not loving, forgiving, compassionate, in peace with yourself and the whole universe, when you are not true to yourself and to other, and when you wait until God is all you have left, before you know that He is all you need, then your life will be a failure because you missed the main raison of your human experience. And you will be "punished" by your deeds and not for your deeds.

So God is not someone or something to fear but to love.

There is more respect in love than in fear.

The power of God is hidden in His love. And when I discovered that He was "only love" because He is perfect, then I could love Him without fear or expectation. It was a different kind of love which was unconditional not only from Him but from me too. I understood that He does not force me to worship Him or do what He says, but He gave me free will. And I choose to love Him not to avoid punishment or get reward, but because it feels good, it's fulfilling.

No matter what they may have tell you all your life about things you have to do or not do to deserve His love, "know" that His love is unconditional, so let yours be unconditional.

And remember that if Love is the treasure, forgiveness is the key to the treasure.

12

◄○►

The Story Of The Repentant Sinner And The Two Sages

This Story is very well known in Islam but little understood.

A man that murdered 98 persons in his life decided one day to repent and start a new life, but he did not know what to do. There were two highly respected learned men in the village where he lives and he decided to ask them. He went to the first one and told him that he has not been in the right path and had in fact killed a total of 98 persons, but now wants to repent and do good deeds the rest of his life. The learned man told him that there was no chance that he could be forgiven, because God was very clear in the scriptures, and that he will go to Hell because of his sins. The sinner told him: "ok then I can just take your life as well" and he did so to make him the 99 victims.

He then decided to go to the other learned man and told him the same story. The man told him: "ok my son God is merciful and if you are really sincere in your path to change, He will forgive all your sins, but you have to go to a place where you never sinned before and when you get there, you ask for forgiveness from you heart and He will forgive you."

The man was so content with the possibility that even him could be forgiven, that he decided to find that place. He had to make a very long journey because he almost sinned everywhere.

In his way into finding this place, he died. When the Angels brought him to God, they were very concerned for his fate because he did not reach the place and the distance travelled was less than the remaining distance. But God's verdict was that he will be forgiven all his sins because of his genuine intention and is willingness to change.

The first learned man by preaching a punishing God lost his life and was proven wrong by God because the sinner was forgiven. And only God knows if he (the learned man) will not have to experience one way or another, the consequences of his lack of wisdom, by preaching a punishing God and discouraging someone who have decided at last to return to his creator.

The second learned man in his wisdom and understanding of the spirit of the Scriptures, not the content, preached a Merciful God and was proven right. He knew how disconnected this man has been all his life and how bad his actions were in the side of God, but he also knew that the heart of the Lord is mercy and that He always accept a "repentant soul".

And the wisdom behind telling the sinner to find a place he never sinned before and to ask for forgiveness was to test his commitment, because he knew that he had to travel far.

This story is very symbolic, because it teaches us that God is "The Lord of Mercy" and that we should not understand, preach, teach or tell about God anything other than hope, forgiveness and love.

And the second message is that to change we don't need to travel but you do need to be truly committed and to take the step toward the change.

13

The Learned

To search for knowledge is one of the highest priorities of our existence, the knowledge of ourselves, of God and the Universe. Indeed the first word the Angel Gabriel told the Prophet Muhammad (pbuh) in "Mount Hira" where he received the revelation that started his Prophecy, was "Ikhra" in Arabic, which means: "Read". And this is the verse:

"Read! In the name of your Lord and Cherisher,

Who created-created man, out of a (mere) clot of congealed blood,

Read! And your Lord is most bountiful,

He who taught (the use of) the pen,

Taught man what he knew not."

The Angel Gabriel did not tell him to pray or to worship. It was read, and to read is to learn.

There is a divine wisdom in this verse, because it says that all knowledge comes from the creator.

But it began by telling you to learn, you have to seek the knowledge before it is given to you.

However knowledge is just a collection of information and we need discernment for the knowledge that we acquire by learning. We need wisdom, to see through "The eyes of God". And that is what Albert Einstein meant when he said: "I want to know God's thoughts; the rest are details." When you know the way "God thinks" then you have both knowledge and wisdom and then you can understand things the way they are supposed to be understood. But to act upon knowledge without wisdom can be very dangerous. In fact human history is full of testimony about that.

Adolf Hitler madness was derived from an ideology of a superior race based upon knowledge from great thinkers. Communism was an ideology from great thinkers but without wisdom.

The crusades were inspired and called to reclaim the control of the Holy Land of Jerusalem by the Pope who was supposed to be a symbol of wisdom and the teaching of Jesus. Most of the extreme views that some Muslims (and Christians, Jews, Hindus) have, are inspired by great scholars who became voice of authority because of their supposed knowledge of the Scriptures. They can be very dangerous because they don't always have the wisdom to see through "God's eyes" and grasp the spirit of the message instead of the content, but also because they can lose humility, their ego can take them over to the point of giving them divine right over their fellow human beings.

It was the learned of Israel who have tried and convicted Jesus based on their interpretation of the Scriptures, the fear of losing their power and Caiaphas argument that: "Is better for one man to died for the people, than all nation to perish." But that argument was just an alibi because in the contrary the message of Jesus was to resurrect the nation. They used the words of God to put to death a messenger of God.

God wants us to seek knowledge but He wants it to be our own knowing, our own experience.

Do not take others people conclusion to be your reality. If you are sincere in your search, God will reveal Himself to you. God wants us all to discover Him. Knowledge is not wisdom.

And as Albert Einstein said: "Great spirits have always found violent opposition from mediocrities. The latter cannot understand it when a man does not thoughtlessly submit to hereditary prejudices but honestly and courageously uses his intelligence."

14

<hr>

An Eye For An Eye

What if the deeper meaning of "An eye for an eye" is that what you send into the universe is what you will get back, no less, no more and not an invitation to take revenge and do unto others what they have done to you. A God who makes it clear that He is Merciful can not instruct you to do the opposite of what He is. A forgiving God can not teach revenge.

So to interpret "An eye for an eye" as permission or divine right to be as bad as the bad, just not more, is very human. But if you can appeal to the image of God within you which is your spirit that does not carry any "baggage", no judgment, no pain and no ego, then you can understand that the wisdom behind it, is that if you do something bad it will come back to you. "What you sow you reap" because what you do to others, you do to yourself. In reality when you can go beyond the illusion of separation you will find that you and "the others" are one and the same.

If someone hurts you, you don't need to hurt him back, because he will have to experience the consequences of his deeds and you don't need to be involve in that process of Karma.

You will not be punished for your deeds but by your deeds and all the Prophets and the great Masters know that.

Jesus knew about the Ten Commandments, but when he was asked about the fate of the woman accused of adultery, he did not say, "Stone her to death because that is what God said in the Scriptures". He said, "Let those who have never sinned throw the first stone". And nobody did, because he made them face their own consciousness like a mirror and they could see that they were all sinners and wished to be forgiven. It was the oldest that left the scene first, followed by the youngest that were more zealot, probably not even knowing the full meaning of what they were about to do. When they all left Jesus asked her: "is it anybody here to judge you?" she said: "no" and Jesus told her: "I also do not condemn you, go and sin no more".

If Jesus who was the spirit of the Scriptures did not judge her, it is because God did not judge her. She became a follower of Jesus, an example of righteousness and a teacher of Jesus message.

The Prophet Muhammad (pbuh) was disapproved, humiliated, persecuted, attempted to be killed, forced to exile and fought for more than ten years. Many of his companions and followers were tortured or killed in very atrocious ways by Abu Sufian and his army. But when the truth prevailed at the end, the Prophet returned to Mecca from his exile in Medina with an army of ten thousand to proclaim that, "there is only one God and Muhammad (pbuh) is his messenger", Abu Sufian, his wife Hind that ordered the killing of the Prophet's uncle, Hamza, in a very barbaric way, and all the Meccans that fought against the Prophet were scared that they may be executed in retaliation. But the Prophet ordered that the life of Abu Sufian and his wife Hind and their belonging should be safe, and that nobody should be killed and no tree should be cut.

The Prophet Muhammad (pbuh) did not practice "an eye for an eye" and he knew the spirit of the Koran more than anyone because it came through him and he lived it, He was the spirit.

And it was forgiveness, in another word "God" that he practiced and that forgiveness won the heart and mind of those who were still resisting his message and united the all country under one faith: Islam which is a religion of peace.

If the Dalai Lama and Nelson Mandela are among the "Mahatmas" (great souls) of our time, is because of their ability to dismiss any idea of revenge after all they went through and have the wisdom to forgive. There is something in our humanism that admires people that can forgive, because they remind us of God.

Gandhi said it all: "An eye for an eye will leave the all world blind"

Forgiveness is the spirit of all religions for anyone that is willing to see it.

If you want to know the spirit of a message, look at the messenger more than the message, because you may not understand the depth and the wisdom of the message.

But your destination is not the message or the messenger.

15

◄O►

Stepping Stone

The messenger and the message are both stepping stones. The messenger is trying to tell you to look at his way of being, his state of mind and the miracles he can accomplish, and to understand that it is because he has connected himself to something. He is saying: "I got this power by tapping into the source of all power and that you can get the same power if you get to where I am."

No true messenger ever claimed to have a personal power that is accessible to him only, or to be worshiped. In fact they always try to make it clear that they are not important, that it is not about them, and that their purpose is just to awaken us to the illusion of this world.

They want their life to be a witness to what lay beyond the visible into the world of the invisible where everything emanates. It's just like someone standing and pointing to something extraordinary in the sky, but the person pointing is so beautiful and special that your eyes are directed and focus on him instead of what he is trying to show you.

Many people spend their all life marvelling the beauty and the miracles of the pointer and never really look at what he is pointing to.

Your destination is what the messenger is pointing to and when you get there you will be as "beautiful" and miraculous as he is.

Do not spend more time than necessary in the pointer, you have to look at him just the time to witness his beauty, but remember that his state of consciousness and all the miracles he accomplished are an effect and the cause is what he is pointing to, and that is the being which is the source of everything. The "Alpha and the Omega" of creation, the mysterious being that all the Prophets, the sages, the masters and even a growing number of the science community are pointing to, He is refers to in the Koran as: "ALLAH". There is a chapter in the Koran call "AL-IKHLAS," or Purity (of faith), that talks about that being. And it says: "In the name of Allah, the Most Gracious Most Merciful.

1. "Say; He is Allah,
   The One and Only

2. Allah, the Eternal, Absolute;

3. He begetteth not,
   Nor is He begotten;

4. And there is none
   Like unto Him."

The Prophet Muhammad (pbuh) had said that this short chapter is one third of the entire Koran.

The Hindu Holy Book the Bhagavad-Gita speaking about this being said: "He is the Source of the Material and the Spiritual world, everything emanates from Him."

We call it different names but we are obviously talking about the same being. And the number one priority in our life is to seek and find Him in our life and in ourselves. When through the message or the messenger you are be able to access the "Source", then the messenger has fulfilled his mission and the message have been received and understood.

Let us try to be like the messenger and access his consciousness. In any given moment in life we can ask ourselves, what would have done the messenger of the path that I am following? And you will find that only love and compassion is their message. Don't try to do what the followers of that particular faith are doing because many of them are not following the footsteps of their Masters. And that is what Gandhi meant when he said: "I like your Christ but I do not like your Christians. Your Christians are so unlike your Christ". Gandhi was a real "Christian" if Christian means Christ like. He did not speak about religion, he lived it. He indeed lived out the teaching of the "Sermon on the Mount". Nonviolence is one of the teachings of Jesus that Gandhi understood and practiced more than many baptised and bible expert. And Passive resistance is what Jesus personified in the trial that crucified him, he did not try to defend or protect himself against the Jewish council or Pontus Pilatus. In fact he said words he knew would condemn him and he kept the spirit of his teaching until the end. And that is why his spirit is still alive.

16

All Religions Are True

(In essence)

One of the pillars in Islam is to believe in all the Prophets and their have been many according to Islam. One "Hadith" puts the number at 124000 (Ibn Hanbal Musnad, 5, 169).

The Koran says: "There never was a people without a warner having lived among them (35:24)" The Koran even makes it clear that some are mentioned in the Koran and some are not. The pillar is not only saying that they have existed and they were sent or inspired by God, but most importantly that they brought a path that is different from yours.

This pillar says clearly to us that God has shown himself to them all in different ways and that they had spoken to people about their path. The different paths should be seen as divine wisdom. People are different and that is why the roads should also be different for each of us to find the one that speaks to us best, the one that appeals more to our uniqueness and leads us to the SOURCE which is the goal.

We should not only respect but "know" that other paths are as "true" and "perfect" as ours in essence because they all come from the only one God that has chosen to express Himself in different ways.

If I take the analogy of Water (H_2O) to represent God (the Source), wherever you go in the world the atomic structure of water will be two atoms of Hydrogen bonded to one atom of Oxygen. We have given it different names in different part of the world and in different languages:

- In Swedish (Vatten)
- In French (Eau)
- In Swahili (Maji)
- In Latin (Aqua)
- In Wolof (Ndokh)

But all the different names point to the same substance (H_2O) that is essential to life, it is a major constituent of all life forms, most animals and plants contain 60% of that substance by volume, and the human body can be up to 70% made of it. Without this substance life would have probably never developed on our planet.

Now if my experience of this vital and miraculous substance is through the name "Ndokh", since I was born I never heard anyone call it anything other than that, then for me that substance can not be other than "Ndokh".

If I meet a Swedish and we see the substance "H_2O" and I tell him that this substance is very important in life and his name is "Ndokh", and he says that he knows this substance better than me and the name is "Vatten", we then start to argue about the name because we experienced it through different name but we are both right because in essence we are talking about the same thing "H_2O". I don't need to force him to start calling it what I call it or to say that he must be talking about something else because the divine name of "H_2O" is "Ndokh".

There is only one substance in the Universe that has the atomic structure of H_2O. It can appear in different forms (gas, liquid, solid) and we can give it different names but his attributes and properties will be the same.

The name you give a thing is not the thing.

If we replace Water H2O with God, we can see that we are doing the same thing about God because If I happened to be born in Senegal, into a Muslim family, most probably my experience of what we call God will be through Islam: "That there is only one God and Muhammad (pbuh) was send by Him, that He (God) is omniscient, omnipotent and omnipresent, Merciful and His name is Allah".

Now if I meet a French who was born and grew up in a Christian family where it is believed that Jesus is not only God's son but the Lord Himself, for him Jesus has all the attributes of God, all knowing, Omnipotent, Omnipresent and Merciful.

Together we meet a Jewish who considers himself belonging to the "chosen people" and calling God "Yahweh". And we all three meet a "Jehovah's witness" that says that the name of God is "Jehovah".

If we were sitting around a table and try to talk about God, what would most likely happen is that each of us would think that he has the truth in his side because of his personal and "special experience". He would not have the wisdom to consider that other may have a different experience but as true as his. And from his belief of having the exclusive truth, he would think that God is with him and not with the others. Now from his mental position, he would take it personal and see it as a divine duty to convince the others that they were wrong and should better join the truth if they wish to be saved from the flame of Hell. He would insist that the sacred name of God is what he calls it and not what they call it.

In short we would argue about God's "real name", which book is the word of God, which religion is God's religion, which way we should pray. We would try hard to divide unconsciously the One God that we share.

The Koran warned us to respect the "People of the book" because their books come from God. Some learned will argue that they agree about the fact that "others" book originally comes from God, but the message became distorted, some verses were changed, and their book has been corrupted. But this is where they missed the all point, or lacked the wisdom that learning can not provide.

The Koran speaks about the spirit of the book. God is spirit therefore always talking about the spirit of things not their content. The Spirit of all holy books is true. Do not spend time trying to find differences instead see the eternal truths hidden in all of them.

There are many learned men from different religions spending most part of their life trying to prove wrong all other religions. They can study other religious books or spiritual paths searching for differences in the content. They are agents of separation, they are not serving God, but they can not see it because they are so identified with their mental position and have to defend it in any cost be it denying the truth. It has become personal and is not about God anymore, is about them being right. It is vanity and vanity is not God.

If we can go out of our mental position for a moment, forget all we have learned and the prejudices we have about "other". If we can "empty our mind" we will see, as a moment of absolute truth that we are talking about the same being with the same attributes: Omniscient, Omnipotent, Omnipresent, Loving and Merciful.

Some separating entity, in their ego driven search had come out with the theory that the Buddha was influenced by the teachings of Hinduism, or that Jesus was in Asia in his "lost years" to learn and to take with him the teachings of the Buddha and that the Prophet Muhammad (pbuh) came in contact and was inspired by the teachings of Moses (Torah) and Jesus (the Gospel).

They choose to see a conspiracy in the similarity of their basic teachings. But what they are unconsciously saying is that their teachings came from the same source.

The name we give to God, which one of his messengers has enlightened us, the path we take, the way we pray and our rituals are not the destination. God is the destination. And not only the concept of God but the experience of God and that experience is different from people to people, culture to culture, religion to religion, but all equally valuable and true.

As far I am concerned, I am to the best of my ability, "completely submitted to the will of God" which is the meaning of Islam. I pray as the prophet Muhammad (pbuh) prescribes it every day, but I meditate too everyday. I don't have any problem going to a Church, a Synagogue, a Temple because to me they are all like a Mosque: a house build for the remembrance of God. But I also know that the God you are seeking in those places is at home and even closer, inside you.

The Koran says that the Prophets Abraham and Jesus were Muslims because they were completely submitted to the will of God, and that is all that matters, not the way we pray or if you go to the Mosque, the Temple, the Synagogue or the Church or if you just "be" and feel God.

If you understand the essence of Islam you will know that anyone who is submitted to the will of God (which is love, peace, truth, compassion, justice, forgiveness and oneness), is your Muslim brother or sister.

The more you understand your own path by committing to the spirit of it not the content, the more you see the oneness with other paths. Some will argue that their way is the only "right one" and other will accept that there are other "right" ways but their path is the best or fastest.

But God is all the ways and if you denied one you denied all. Diversity is nature plan, is something to celebrate and not to argue about. We are Different branches of the same tree. Diversity is nothing but an expression of oneness. It is in fact one of lives conditions because if we all whistled the same note there would be no music.

We are the world and God is watching us to see what we will make of it. He has given us all the power, knowledge and free will to create the destiny we want for ourselves and our planet.

We can keep our uniqueness and together join our shared values in a place were spirituality will be the common denominator.

17

From Religion To Spirituality

When I got the clarity that all religions are true in essence and further to the fact that "Religion is made for Men and not Men for Religion", it became obvious to me that a human being is more important than any religion or all religions put together.

You are so dear to God that He sent Messengers with messages to remind you who you truly are and guide you back to Him, even though you never left because your very essence, your soul is a part of Him and can not exist outside of Him.

It is said that "Men is made in the image of God", not good men, great men, or saints, but all men. It is this image of God that makes all men special. If you can see God in all human beings, then you have understood the essence of your religion and you would see that you can never use religion to hurt, be enemy, or even dislike someone because the person does not share your beliefs, ideologies or methods. Islam says that "if you kill one person, you kill the whole humanity", this is how important you are: The whole is in the part and the part is the all.

Religion is not synonymous, or equal to God. God is everything.

Religion is a wonderful tool that can, if used properly, guide you to the Source, but if misunderstood can be the worse evil known to man, because of the conviction that you are serving God. Which echo the wisdom of Vaclav Havel words: "Keep the company of those who seek the true and run from those who found it."

You can be very religious and very evil, the saying: "Close to the Church, far from God", is very common.

The Prophet Muhammad (pbuh) said: "Islam is a way of life". Is not about what you do on Fridays at the Mosque or on Sundays at Church, at the Synagogue or the Temple, is what you say and do when those moments are over, is all about your interaction with the entire Universe.

Are you giving love to your wife, to your husband, to your children, your parents, your friends, co-workers, people you don't know, to animals, nature? Are you peaceful or violent in words and deeds? Are you faithful in relationship? Are you an agent of harmony and reconciliation or discord?

"The Greatest among you are those who serve others" not those who pray the most, not the one that is mostly in meditation, not the learned one. "If you want to serve God, serve people", said the Prophet Muhammad (pbuh). God is already what he is: Perfect. He does not need our devotion because it does not add anything to Him and if you don't, it can not take away anything from Him.

Your services don't matter to Him, but they do matter to people who needs it and to yourself in return. Buddha, Krishna, Lao Tzu, Confucius, Abraham, Moses, Jesus and Muhammad (pbuh) and other enlightened messengers did not lock themselves in a room separated from the world with their enlightenment, praying and meditating all day everyday, because they understood that in the words of Confucius: "We work our humanity in our interaction with people, a yogi, 40 years in the mountain, is not serving unless he comes down and share."

The return to oneself is necessary, but the opening to the world is the ultimate goal.

God is serving us all the time, in fact one the greatest quality of God is giving, He still gives to those who denied His existence, when the sun shine to give life he does not choose good people, he shines for all. The rain does not choose the houses in which it is poured. Life is not about having but giving, and to all not only those nearest to you or those who share your beliefs and ideologies. The question should not be how you can become somebody so that you can be served but rather, how you can find yourself so that you can share your wisdom, be at service and remind people what they have forgotten which is what they really are. And to access that level of awareness you can ask the big question: "Who am I".

When you ask that question, you may find out that you are not your name, you are not your race, you are not your gender, you are not your religion, and not even your body.

You do have a name, your skin have a colour, you live in a female or a male body, and you may have a religion, but you are not those things; you have them.

So who is the "YOU" that have those things? "YOU" is Spirit. You are Spirit.

The moment the spirit leaves the body, you will still have your name, you will still be black or white, you will be buried according to your faith and your body will be there but "YOU" is not there anymore. So all the time "YOU", was not all those things. "YOU" was never visible.

When you ask who "Am I", you will only discover who you are not, but that is all you need to know. When you take away what you are not, then you will be left with what you are. When the illusion is gone, reality will shine because it has been hidden by the veil of what is not real.

When you come to the conclusion that you are Spirit, then you can see that in reality you are not different from anybody else because all that differentiates you from other is not what you are, while what you are, you share with everybody else. When you get to that level of awareness, then you understand what Jesus meant when he said: "Love your neighbor as yourself", because in essence you and your neighbor are the same. You are your neighbor.

The Prophet Muhammad (pbuh) also said: "Unless you desire for your neighbor what you desire for yourself, you don't have faith". He also said: "A man going to bed his belly full while his neighbor is hungry is not a Muslim".

They tried to warn us about the illusion of separation. They tried to wake us up to the reality of oneness. We are spirit, and spirit is one. All spirit is derived from one spirit which is God. This is why Spirituality which is the study of the spirit is where we should all meet no matter what religion you belong to, or if you are an Atheist, an Agnostic or just a scientist.

We can keep our religion and our practices, but just be aware and get to the realization of oneness. Let us accept positive changes, flexibility is a sign of wisdom. Be like water. As Mahatma Gandhi said: "A true disciple knows another's woes as his own, he bows to all and despise none."

18

The Image Of God

The discovery that you are a "spiritual being having a human experience" and not a "human being having a spiritual experience", have a tremendous implication in your perception and the entire process of creating your life. If you unconsciously think that you are your body and read in the Scriptures that: "Man was created in the image of God", you will automatically, with the help of human history of prejudices and misinterpretations, think that God must be a old white man. And your natural concept of Him would be the likeness of a king which is someone to fear and please, because susceptible of being angry, jealous, selfish, controlling and punishing those who do not obey his laws or follow his will". Because a king depends on people to keep his power and privileges. If people decided to overthrow him, he would lose his power. He does not have a power of his own. But if you "know" that you are spirit living in a body, you will assume that God is spirit also, because you are made in his image, and not a king with human attributes.

From that awareness you would stop associating Him with human weaknesses like anger, jealousy, revenge, punishment, resentment and the whole stream of negative emotions.

Because humans live in a body, they will be subject to those weaknesses. But when they elevate their consciousness to transcend the body and let the image of god shine, then only love will be left. Because love is the ultimate reality, is the nature of God.

To think or preach a punishing God is the reflection of our own human state of being is "to create God in the image of man".

God is spirit so are we, and that understanding unveils a power that his within you, that has been given to you from creation, that power his dormant within you and is your own essence.

All the Prophets and the great Masters spoke about a mysterious force located inside every human being, some call it "the Buddha inside", some call it "Christ consciousness" and in the Scriptures God said: "Neither Earth or Heaven can contain Me but the heart of My servant." Also: "If you find Me not within you, you will never find Me; for I have been with you from the beginning." Rumi the great Sufi poet said: "You have been created with wings, why prefer to crawl?"

Many human beings crawl through life because they are not aware of their wings, other in fear of living their comfort zone and what they may discover, and many because of their belief systems. However, the truth is that God wants us to fly.

Enlightened human beings in all religions have been trying to awaken us to this fact but the "Learned" have tried and succeeded to suppress it in organized religions which most of the time reflect the structures of the human ego with hierarchy, domination, control and misinterpretation of the words of God. There are many genuine Imams, Rabbis, Priests, Gurus, or spiritual teachers, that would have the sincerity to let you know that what you are seeking in them or what you respect them for is also in you, and that you just haven't used it or developed it.

That "the power is within you" is in fact the Depth and spirit of religion. Religion was meant to free people not enslave them, but make them realise their own potential and the infinite possibility of universal love.

The Prophet Muhammad (pbuh) always tried to remind people that he was just a human, not to be worshiped, and at the same time showed us from what he has accomplished, how powerful humans can become when they are willing to go within and find the image of God, and used it to change themselves and the world. Jesus always said: "what I can do, you can do too and more"

And when he said "I and the Father are one", he did not mean that he(Jesus) was the creator of Heaven and Earth, but simply that he was created in the image and spirit of God. And he was aware of it and did use it to testify the power of God.

Do not underestimate yourself because if you do, you underestimate God, because the image of God that is your essence has to be powerful. The world has been shaped by the power of "One", God never send a group of messenger, it only takes one human being to give birth to a idea or a intention that ultimately will resonate in the hearts of others and change the world.

The potential to change yourself and the world around you has been given to you from birth.

Stop doubting yourself and "fear no evil" because the Lord is with you all the time.

19

Fear & Doubt

(THE HIDDEN SIDE OF THINGS)

Fear is considered to be human beings worst enemy, it is the cause of so many unfulfilled dreams, limitations, regrets, prejudices, wars, psychological and physical diseases. It is a force that has terrorised human since the beginning of time. Is an energy that exists in the Universe and comes in a form of thoughts to all human beings, but it appears in your life:

- to make you think different, change your belief systems.
- to challenge you, test your commitment.
- to make you become better than you used to be.
- to raise your level of awareness.

The saying that "fear is just an illusion", if misinterpreted, can be very damaging because you may think that it does not "exist" and therefore ignore it, and we know that whatever we are not conscious about we can not control. According to both Science and Spirituality, the material world as we know it is an illusion. But we still have to deal with it, we can not ignore it or pretend that is not there because it "exist". The same thing is true about fear, it is "a real illusion", not just an illusion that weak and ignorant people have created or are subjected to, but an energy that "great people" also are exposed to. Make no mistake, great people feel fear but their greatness is that they don't let it stop them, because if it does not paralyze or "destroy" you, it will make you stronger.

If you studied the life of Muhammad Ali the legendary heavyweight boxer spiritually, you will see that what made him great were not his boxing skills and his words, but his spirit. And the main aspect of his spirit was the way he dealt with fear. Many may think that he never felt fear because they never saw it in his face but when after the death of Sonny Liston he was asked: "if you could talk to him now what would you say to him?", he answered: "you scared me to death". And that is the truth that we need to know so that we may learn something from him. He was not immune from fear and that does not take away anything from his greatness, in the contrary it should make him even greater in our eyes because his life shows that there is a way to conquer fear and become whatever we want to be. All the experts agreed about the odds being 7-1 for Sonny Liston in 1964 and 3-1 with George Foreman in 1974 in Zaire Africa. But what they did not know was Muhammad Ali state of mind. He dealt with the energy of fear by facing it, feeling it and letting it go. His tactic was to visit his opponent's training ground, to see him life face to face, probably to feel the "fear", not to resist it or be in a denial. He was also known to talk a lot about how good and handsome he was and how and why he was going to win. But that attitude had nothing to do with arrogance in fact those who knew him personally would testify that he was a humble, loving and spiritual human being. It was indeed a sense of humour and entertainment in his attitude and his words, but I think that Ali was using the power of word consciously or unconsciously, because his words did more harm to the psychic of his opponent than his punches to their bodies. His words transferred the negative energy of fear to his opponent's consciousness. Both Sonny Liston and George Forman started doubting before the fights because they felt and the whole world felt with them that Ali was supposed to be scared and apparently was not. And that attitude made them scared instead.

Muhammad Ali is in fact a very enlightened human being who walked his spiritual path in the boxing world. The lessons to learn from a person that really personify the power of positive affirmation "I am the greatest" is that he used to feel fear even if apparently people could not see it (and that is important too, because if his opponent could see it, it wouldn't have any effect) but he was not in a state of superficial denial either, because if you make a positive affirmation and do not believe in it deep in your subconscious, because of what "fear is telling you", you will still vibrate the opposite of what you are affirming and your opponent will feel it.

Muhammad Ali was very confident, and confidence is not the absence of fear, but to have a faith that is bigger than your fears. He indeed had a strong faith. When a journalist tried to make fun of him before his fight with George Forman and said that "Ali only had a prayer", he answered by saying: "All I need is a prayer because when a prayer reach the right man, not only Forman will fall but mountains will fall". But fear will still visit you even with this kind of faith.

Do not associate with fear, is not you. But do not fight it, is not your enemy. His real purpose is not to destroy you but to warn you to train yourself more, to seek more knowledge, to change the way you think, to be a better you before you seek something better.

Fear can be seen as a challenge to overcome so that you can grow and be prepared for things you are not equipped to handle now. His hidden message is the opportunity it gives you to rise and when you see it that way and face it, feel it and release it, then it will mutate to become an asset to you.

When Rosa Park was asked to give away her seat in a bus to a white man because of her race that fateful day of December 1, 1955, and that they called the police to remove and arrest her, she surely felt fear because she was defying a law and not the whim of a bus driver or a passenger, but rather a system. However by refusing to give her seat, she transcended the barriers of fear. So it is not the absence of fear, but the fact that she acted despite it against all odds that made her special.

When she made the choice to do the right thing by refusing injustice, she removed the barriers of fear in the consciousness of the black community and that simple act led to the civil right movement.

When you go through fear, his energy mutates and there is nothing that can stop the new energy which is build when the barriers of fear are broken. And that energy is in fact what is hidden behind fear.

Gandhi was told to move to the Van Compartment in a train to Pretoria in South Africa while having a first class ticket just because he was a "coloured man". He refused and was thrown out of the train, with his luggage, by a police man in a very cold winter day. When Gandhi was challenged the second time in that same journey by a white man to give him his seat, and in spite of knowing that he could be thrown out again, he said: "I, trembling said no". He said in his own words how much he felt the energy of fear, but what changed everything was his ability to do the right thing while scared. He later said: "my experience in the train to Pretoria changed my life." Indeed That day the barriers of fear were broken in his consciousness and that led to all his later achievements and his footprints in human history.

The secret is not to get to a place where there is no fear, but to be able to act and pursue your goal or just do the right thing despite the feeling of fear.

Doubt and fear are different face of the same coin. They vibrate at the same frequency and just like fear doubt has a hidden message. In fact doubt is necessary in life, without doubt there can be no faith. Faith is to believe when there is doubt, and not the absence of doubt.

Doubt is one of the components of faith, because to have faith you need two things: "doubt and belief". Note that if you are in your comfort zone the energy of doubt will not manifest in your life. And if you don't have any doubt you should know that you are not evolving, you are not exploring new horizons, you are probably doing things the way you used to with what you always knew and with the same outcome. You take no risk because of fear of the unknown.

But when you want to know what life has in store for you, when you seek higher ground, want to discover your purpose in life and ready to leave your comfort zone with all the challenges it may involve to fulfil your dreams, then you should understand that in reality you need doubt, because is a sign that you are, or about to be in new territory. You should welcome it and don't resist it, be aware of it, embrace it, and go through it but do not mistake it to be who you are.

With doubt you have one of the components toward your greatness. He is testing you he wants to pull you out of your comfort zone to explore the unknown, the realm of the invisible where everything is created before it takes shape in the visible world.

Doubt is the barrier, the wall between the small you and the big you, the real you and the false you. His purpose is to force you to rise to that divine place call faith, where you go beyond your five senses and your raison. Use it positively act while feeling doubtful, and his energy will mutate and together with belief give birth to the miracle of what we call Faith.

The Prophets had their moment of doubt and all the great and successful people have been subject to that energy. In religion it's called "the dark night of the soul".

The Prophet Muhammad(pbuh) was attacked and submerged by the energy of doubt when he first received the divine revelation that started his prophecy in Mount Hira by Arc Angel Gabriel.

The darkness and ignorance of his society, the condition of the poor, the deplorable situation of women, who were treated worse than animals, the excess of wine drinking, gambling, murder, torture and the immorality in people behaviour tormented his soul. He would then retire to a cave located at the top of the mountain called "Mount Hira" to meditate and find peace of mind for his trouble heart. One day while he sat in the cave. "Angel Gabriel" the angel of revelation appeared to him and said: "Recite!" He said in surprise "I can not read", again the divine voice stated "Recite, O Muhammad", He replay: "what shall I recite". And the voice for the third time repeated, "Recite in the name of your Lord who created.

He created the man from a clot,

Recite and your Lord is most honourable,
Who taught (to write) with the pen
Taught the human being what he knew not."

The Prophet was in tremendous fear after receiving the revelation. He run home to his wife Khadidja, trembling, sweating, scared and thought he was possessed by demons, because he did not see himself, a small illiterate Bedouin, worthy of being chosen for a great purpose. It was Khadidja who told him that a man of his character and heart can not be touch by evil forces. But that could not take away his doubts then Khadidja took him to her uncle "Warakha" an old Jewish man who now was blind but was very familiar with the Scriptures. And it was indeed Warakha who told Muhammad (pbuh) and Khadidja that it was indeed "Gabriel" the angel of revelation that talked to him, and that he has been chosen as was Abraham, Moses, Jesus and all the Prophets before them to deliver a message from God. After that conversation the Prophet Muhammad (pbuh) started to believe in himself and in his message with all his being.

Remember the bigger the doubt, the bigger the faith will be, when you can add belief to your doubt.

Whenever the voice of greatness is calling, the first answer is always no. Even the greatest among us, even those who became messengers always started by doubting themselves.

We are all afraid of our greatness. Moses was doubtful when God talked to him in the "burning bush of Mount Sinai". He did not think of himself worthy of being addressed and chosen by God to deliver a message to Pharaoh and to set his people free, he a shepherd in the run from Egypt. And it was his brother Aaron that reminded him of who he was.

When the Prophet Jeremiah was called his answer was: "I am too young".

When Mary the mother of Jesus was told that she was chosen to be part in an extraordinary event in human history, her answer was: "How could that be, I have never been with a man".

When the Prophet Isaiah was called, his answer was: "I am unclean".

So do not take it personal if doubt occurs in your life, it wants you to bring out faith.

To believe is to say "yes I don't know yet but I am willing to try to the best of my ability". There is no certainty in believe but that is the test, because if you can be comfortable with not knowing for certain, feeling doubtful and still going forward, still acting with integrity and vision, the miracle of Faith will be in motion. Seemingly bad things are in reality serving a good purpose. Beyond the realm of opposite everything is positive and for the evolution of the Universe.

In the big picture everything has is reason to be, negative feelings or circumstances are serving a good purpose, if you can face them they will tell you something. They are calling you to something greater. Have the courage to answer the calling.

20

---◄〇►---

Courage

When you choose to act despite fear and doubt, a new energy is born that vibrates in a different and higher frequency and that energy is what we call courage.

Courage is an act of faith. Is when you say yes to life, to the impulse of the Universe against all odds with uncertainty to the vastness of the unknown, you conspire with life to bring about something better. The universe is always searching for a channel, a vessel, to bring about change. Whenever a soul is ready to be used, the Divine intelligence will use it. That is why when you are courageous enough to do the right thing, to choose peace instead of war, justice instead of corruption, self- realisation instead of self- sacrifice, love instead of hate, forgiveness instead revenge, something greater than you, more powerful than you can ever imagine existed, will be set in motion. You are not alone anymore even if at the beginning it may seem that way.

By being courageous you may lose many things, go through the dark night of the soul: when you feel abandoned, lonely, opposed.

You may even think that what you did was wrong, while you deep inside know that it is right. When you are in the tunnel before the light appear , you may regret, doubt, condemn yourself, but always remember that an act of courage by doing the right thing can never be wrong. And you can never imagine what the Universe "have in mind". If you are ready to be his instrument your simple act can fulfil the dream of millions.

Just look at what has happened and still happening in some part of the world, where dictators that people used to tremble hearing their names, just lost all their power in a blink of an eye when the barriers of fear and the doubt of uncertainty were broken. These are the miracles of acts of courage.

Rosa Park could never imagine that refusing to give up her seat would set into motion the civil rights movement in United States. She became a role model for courage in the face of racial injustice. She has been chosen by the Universe to be the inspiration for that change; but she did say yes. Great people are not great because they have been chosen, but they are chosen because they already embody particular qualities for that message. Their level of consciousness has to vibrate in a certain frequency, to be picked up, and grace pressed upon them.

To be courageous is to open the door of opportunities and change. You don't need to know the how of things, just be "real" and responsible. And remember that all the big changes throughout human history have not occurred because of armies, nations, or governments. They happened as a result of the courage and commitment of individuals.

Have the courage to speak out for injustice and abuse everywhere. The destiny of our world depends on you. Let us have the courage to create "a mass grave" for greed, prejudices, separation, and extreme ideologies and belief systems.

21

Personal & Collective Responsibility

Gandhi's words: "Be the change you want to see in the world", are so enlightened that they could have come from Confucius, Krishna, Lao Tzu, Buddha, Moses, Abraham, Jesus, Muhammad(peace be upon them all) or any other Prophet or great Master. Human beings have a tendency to blame circumstances, people, and God for every undesirable condition in their life and in the world. But the moment you take responsibility for everything in your life, and your part in the world we have created and most important the world we can create, then you can be an agent for the change you want to see in the world.

To change the world we do need to make it together but the first step is the personal change, because if we all change our own awareness, the collective consciousness will change automatically. The world is a mirror that reflects our collective consciousness. If you want to see a peaceful world, you start by setting an intention to be peaceful in any given moment and circumstances in your life, because the only person you can ever change is you. But by changing, you can inspire your children, spouse, co-workers, friends and even enemy to change. You vibrating peace will change the collective consciousness toward peace.

One of the most fundamental aspects of taking part of the collective responsibility is to not be indifferent to injustice. When a child growing in a family is abused physically or psychologically by his father, receiving no love, no appreciation which ultimately will result in a damaged self-esteem. The mother doesn't react because of fear of the father. At school the child is not doing well, a teacher notice it and clearly see that it must be something wrong at home but choose to be silent instead of taking the necessary steps to involve social workers under the argument that he is just a teacher. The child disappointed by the indifference of the adults, seeks now self destruction in gang member or religious extremism.

The day that child commits a crime, it is indeed the father, the mother, the teacher, the indifferent friends, that helped him to pull the trigger. They are all responsible, because they had a choice to do something and change the course of history. It is not what they did, but what they didn't do.

Is the silence of the good that allows oppression and injustice, it was the silence of the world that allowed Slavery, the Holocaust, Rwanda, and now Darfur. We create injustice and abuse or allowed them to be.

When small children in some part of the world are exploited in child labour, denied education, sexually abused, and we pretend that it is not happening because is not next door. When extreme political or religious ideas take root in a country and people fail to denounce it. When people don't have the courage to take a stand and bring light into darkness, but choose to be silent.

Or complain in their living room doing nothing and expecting that darkness will turn into light one day all by itself. When powerful countries use their power to bring injustice, exploitation and corruption in the world and we choose to be silent because it does not affect us. Then we are all to blame.

Let us be aware of the words of Martin Luther King Junior: "Injustice anywhere is a threat to justice everywhere." An action today can have consequences for generations to come, because even if it does not affect you, people you know or anybody you can think of, you can not see or understand the link and the big picture. We are all connected therefore all responsible for the well being or the misery of one another.

Remember the words of German Anti- Nazi activist, Pastor Martin Niemueller:

> "First they came for the Socialists
> And I did not speak out
> Because I was not a socialist.
> Then they came for the Trade Unionists
> And I did not speak out
> Because I was not a Trade Unionist.
>
> Then they came for the Jews
> And I did not speak out
> Because I was not a Jew
>
> Then they came for me
> And by then there was
> No one left to speak out for me."

22

<hr>

Choice Making

When God gave us free will, He gave us everything. The wisdom of free will if understood can change the world and everything around it.

You don't only have the freedom, which itself is everything because when you are free you can be and do anything, but you also have the power inside you to create your world.

Life does not happen to us, we create it and that is the essence of free will. Your life right now is the sum total of all the choices you have made until this moment, and that is the raison why sometime we say that, "we wished, we did things differently", because we know that we would have a different outcome had we chosen to do things differently. And our world is the sum total of our collective thoughts, feelings and deeds. The Universe is governed by laws, and one of them is cause and effect which states that, "For every action there is an equal and opposite reaction." And we should be grateful that we have the choice and the power to change the cause if we don't like the effect. If you don't like something in your life, a power has been given to you from birth to change it, and most of the time it's about changing the way we see the situation.

There is some directing and controlling power that prevents the Universe from collapsing and that power is supporting you in the co-creation of your life. That power is not conspiring against you, but with you. However it wants you to use your free will. God is not a dictator, neither is He capricious and the Universe is not an obstacle in our path.

You are the producer and the actor of your life and the freedom to choose is the most fantastic tool to be used in the process of co-creation, but it has to be used.

Albert Einstein said: "Nothing happens until something moves." And Quantum physics says the same thing in what is called: "The measurement problem" which states that: "An atom only appears in a particular place if you measure it", in a other word, "a atom is spread all over the place until a conscious observer decide to look at it." What science is saying is that before you look everything is just possibility and will remain so until you "choose" to look, then and only then, a reality is created.

John Wheeler said: "There is no Universe unless there is someone to look at it." The act of observation creates the entire Universe.

The Scriptures say:

- Seek and you should find

- Ask and it shall be given to you

- Knock and it shall be opened to you

Science and religion are saying the same thing, which is that before anything comes to physical existence, a choice or a move has to be made. In Quantum Physics point of view it is the choice of observing that is the cataclysm that will make the wave function of potential to collapse and bring to physical reality what was only possibility. Religion says that before you find, a choice, a move have to be made toward seeking. And that indeed is the decisive moment when you exercise your free will and choose to make the move that will create the reality you prefer.

Use your free will with integrity, is the gift from the divine.

The second layer of both these statements is even more important to understand in our life, and it is hidden for many. The moment we choose to observe, we do not create literally, but we participate in bringing to physical reality something that already existed in another realm.

If something can be both wave and particle according to Quantum Mechanics and the "Copenhagen Interpretation", is because both those realities exist simultaneously in "different frequency".

Religion makes the same assumption in a different language by saying "seek and you will find." It did not say "seek and it will be created", but it says "find" and you can only find something that already exist, that is already created. It is not in your reality now but in another realm and seeking is to search for that different reality in a different vibration. And when you adjust to that frequency, then you have found and it will manifest into your reality.

I like the word co-creator better than creator of our life because everything is already created in different realms and it is for you to decide to bring to physical reality the one you choose.

There is a great wisdom when Science labels their achievements: "Discovery", because we do not create, we only discover some knowledge or natural laws and use that which is already put in place by the only creator there is. We did not create electricity, we discovered his existence and then we created tools to help us use it. When we were not using electricity, it is not because it did not exist, it has existed since the beginning of time, but we were not aware of it. The technology of the internet have always existed, until we discovered it and created ways to use it.

The ultimate wisdom is to be in harmony with creation, and not use your free will against the flow of life. This is what Rumi meant when he said: "Your task is not to seek for love but merely to seek and find all the barriers within yourself you have built against it."

Rumi is saying that what you are looking for already exist. The love you are seeking is inside you, is in fact your essence. You do not have to create anything but to find what is in the way, what is hiding that which already exist, it is a different understanding, a different attitude toward life, and a different vibration. You understand that the Omniscient force of the Universe is your senior partner in the co-creation of your life. Your purpose in life is already created, and is seeking you also, because it wants to be born.

When they asked Michael Angelo how he could create something as beautiful as the sculpture of "David", he said: "David was already in the marble, I just had to release it"

Your "David", is your dreams, your aspirations and the world you want to create and they already exist in the marble, in your consciousness and just like Michael Angelo, you have to feel the marble, to listen and be one with it. Then it will communicate with you and tell you how to remove the barrier to release your greatness. And when "David" comes out, you will be surprise and the world will be surprise.

Use the divine gift of free will to choose to be in harmony with the symphony of the Universe. We are all interconnected and interdependent.

Everything you do or don't do matters. The words you choose to speak, the emotions and feelings you choose to maintain, the actions you choose to take every moment of the day, every day, count. They will guide you toward or away from the source.

Let us stop blaming Satan, each other, Politic, Science and Religion because we are all those things, they don't have a life of their own. And absolutely not blame God when He has given us free will.

23

The Simple Truth
(Oneness)

The statement that "God is one" is the most profound truth in the Universe. That is the spirit of religion and all pathways to enlightenment. The Prophet Muhammad (pbuh) said:

"He (God) is One, One and alone,
He is the only being and there is no
Other being except Him"

GOD IS ONE

There is no two or more rulers or organizers because it is obvious that whatever power or intelligence we call God, the Source and creator of all things has to be one and not many, otherwise the Universe would have been a chaos instead of a Cosmos(harmony).

Even we humans understand and practice that wisdom because all our institutions and organizations must have a leader. We can not have two Kings or two Presidents in the same country and not two "CEO" in the same company.

God is one and One is God, because one is the symbol and mathematical expression of the Source. It is the first incarnation of the totality of consciousness from nothingness, and the one became the whole. Human history has been moved and shaped by the power of one. Even the wisdom of coming together, is to come together as one. When people come together as one, they become God and then everything is possible.

ONE AND ALONE

Unlike humans, God does not need help to create and sustain the Universe, because He is Omniscient, Omnipotent and Omnipresent.

If God is one and alone, this means that He does not have a partner or an opponent, there is no evil force in the Universe which is a counterpart of God. So what is "Satan" and how did he come to existence?

According to the teachings of Islam, what we call "Satan" was a faithful and submitted Angel that has praise God wherever human beings have put their feet. But he rebelled when he was asked to bow before "Adam" the first human being. Because God said that "Adam was going to be made in His (God) image and will be better than everything created before", Angels included.

And the story went on saying that when Adam and Eve were told to not touch the forbidden fruit, they were inspired by Satan to exercise their free will to disobey God and do the opposite of what they were told.

The wisdom in this story, that you don't need to take literally, is that "Satan" was created good. And by "rebelling" which is saying no to God's plan because of his Ego, he created evil.

The best way to make use of this story is to understand that we humans become "Satan" and create "evil" in the world whenever we walk away from God.

The Koran says again that: "All the good that happens to you comes from God and all evil from you." The Koran is making it clear that God did not create evil, God creates only good. He created everything good in the Universe, and everything good you get, you get from Him. But because He had given you free will, and you choose to go away from Him, you will create bad experiences. Nothing bad comes from God and there is no dark power, counterpart of God.

Darkness is the absence of light. When the night falls, it is not because there is a "dark Sun" which is a counterpart of the "light Sun" taking over. There is only one Sun in our planet and it is only good, giving us life and light. And when you don't see it at night, it is not because he isn't there, but because of the rotation of the Earth that hide it and then darkness appears.

The power of "light" is the only real power and it is our own essence, and when we go away from it, we will step into the illusion of the mind that leads to darkness and evil.

The Scriptures did not say: "Let it be light and sometime darkness." No.

God said in the beginning: "Let it be light."

Buddha's enlightenment was that Marat (Satan) was not a counterpart of God, but was purely psychological within us.

We human beings created evil in the world and we have the power within us to choose to create good.

Satan is not an entity sitting somewhere all powerful that we can not escape from.

Some belief system seem to have "have faith in Satan" they will preach the power of the Devil more than the love of God and by listening to their interpretation of the scriptures you may think that at the "Day of Judgment" he (Satan) will succeed to burn more people in "Hell Fire" than God will be able to save with Him in Heaven.

Negatives forces are "real" but it is an energy that we have created with our thoughts, emotions, feelings and actions. That energy is alive and we can choose to give it more power or take away the power we have given it. And the only way we can take away the power is to dwell on the attributes of God: Love, Peace, Truth, Compassion, Justice, Forgiveness and Unity.

Instead of hating Injustice, let us love Justice. It is a different energy.

As Ellen Keller said: "It is wonderful how much time good people spend fighting the Devil, If they would only spend the same amount of energy loving their fellow men, the devil would die in his own tracks of ennui."

HE IS THE ONLY BEING AND THERE IS NO OTHER BEING IN THE UNIVERSE EXCEPT HIM.

This assumption will not make sense as long as you think that you are separated from God.

But in reality every being is an expression of the only being there is. We are spiritual beings coming from the one spirit we call God. One is all and all is one. Everyone is part of the whole and the whole express itself through the part.

All creation is an emanation of God's glory. This is why when you search for yourself you end up finding God and when you search for God you end up finding yourself. Because you and God are not separate and this is what Jesus meant when he said: "I and my father are One.", and not that he (Jesus) is the creator of the Heavens and the Earth.

If you were separated from God, you would not be able to be, nothing can exist outside Him and Science has come to that same conclusion in his one language.

Max Plank, one of the founding father of Quantum Physics, and the Nobel Price winner in1918 said: "All matter originates and exists only by virtue of a force which brings the particle of atom to vibration and holds this most minute solar system of the atom together. We must assume behind this force the existence of a conscious and intelligent mind. This mind is the matrix of all matter."

Modern Science has discovered that in the time of the Big Bang, a field of energy has been displaced. It is invisible and they can not measure it yet, some call it "The mind of God" some "The Container" because it is said that everything in the Universe exist in virtue of that energy. Nothing could exist without it. It permeates and sustains the all Universe.

And Entanglement shows that when two particles of electrons created together are separated, if you subject one to something, the other will react regardless of how far away they are from each other, because they may seem to be in different location, separated in space but energetically they are always connected to each other. And everything was one in the time of the Big Bang.

Oneness is not a beautiful dream or a human utopia, it is now a scientific fact and the spirit of religion has been saying it since the beginning.

You are like a puzzle bit with your name on it, nothing can replace you. You have a special role to play, your uniqueness is what is needed, nothing more nothing less to feet. If you try to be like another part of the puzzle, there will be no use for you anymore because that place is occupied by the one that was designed to fill it in the first place. Without you we will not have the final picture of the puzzle however without the rest you serve no purpose. Every piece of the puzzle is equally important to the concept.

This analogy can be applied to the human race. We are one big family with our physical particularity, but spiritually one spirit, one entity which is the one spirit we call God.

Each of us is a part of the one spirit and when we unite all the parts to one part, we will then at last fulfil our personal and collective life purpose which is to realise God.

It is in the master plan of the Universe (God) that we will be different, but it is a divine wisdom. Diversity is indeed an expression of Oneness and a condition for life. You need different notes to play music.

God is one, does not only mean that we have one God in creation, but that everything is one, because everything is God. He is the totality of consciousness. And that is the absolute truth, the *Simple truth*.

Notes

Muhammad (pbuh): (around 26 of April 570 C.E – 8 June 632)

Mount Hira: is a cave situated in the way to Mina near Mecca and is the place where the Prophet Muhammad (peace be upon him) use to retire and meditate and where he received the revelation that started his prophecy from the Angel Gabriel.

Mecca: is the birth place of the Prophet Muhammad (pbuh) and where Muslims go to pilgrimage. And is where the **Kaaba** the cubed building which is the most sacred site in Islam is located.

Medina: is the place where the Prophet Muhammad (pbuh) is buried his daughter Fatima and the first two leaders of the Muslims after the Prophet Muhammad (pbuh). It was also the place of exile of the Prophet Muhammad (pbhu) and his followers.

Hadith: Is the saying of the Prophet Muhammad (pbuh) which is considered after the reference of Authority after the Koran in Islam.

Khadidja: Was the Prophet Muhammad (pbuh) first wife. She was born in 555 C.E and died in 619 C.E at the age of 64. She was call on of "the mothers of the believers".

Aisha: was a wife of the Prophet Muhammad (pbuh) she was born in 613 C.E and died in 678 C.E in Medina.

Hamza: was the paternal uncle of the Prophet Muhammad (pbuh) and his foster brother. They were raised together as they were almost the same age.

Abu Sufyan: He was born in 560 C.E and died in 650 C.E in Mecca was the leading man in the pagan fight against Islam. He was a fierce opponent of the Prophet Muhammad (pbuh) before accepting Islam later in his life.

Hind: She was the wife of Abu Sufyan.

Warakha: He was the old Jewish blind man that saw the coming of the Prophet Muhammad (pbuh) in the light of the Scriptures.

Rumi: Jalal al.din Rumi was born in 1207 and died in 1273. He was a Persian poet philosopher and Sufi mystic.

Halal: is an Arabic word, which means "lawful".

Caiaphas: He was the Roman-appointed Jewish High Priest who is said to have organised the plot that kill Jesus. Caiaphas is also said to have been involve in the "Sanhedrin" trial of Jesus.

John Archibald Wheeler: He was born in July 9, 1911 and died in April 13, 2008. He was an American theoretical physicist, and a collaborator of Albert Einstein.

Sonny Liston: Charles L. "Sonny" Liston was an American professional boxer and ex convict known for his toughness, punching power and intimidating appearance. He became a world heavyweight champion in 1962 by knocking out Floyd Pattersson in the first round. He died in December 30, 1970.

George Foreman: He was born in January 1949 in Marshall, Texas. He was an American professional boxer who won the heavyweight champion of the world title twice. He is known for the legendary "Rumble in the Jungle" fight against Muhammad Ali in Zaire, Africa, where he lost unexpectedly in the 8 round by knocked out.